APR

D0676807

THE EXTRAORDINARY LIFE OF

STEVE
JOBS

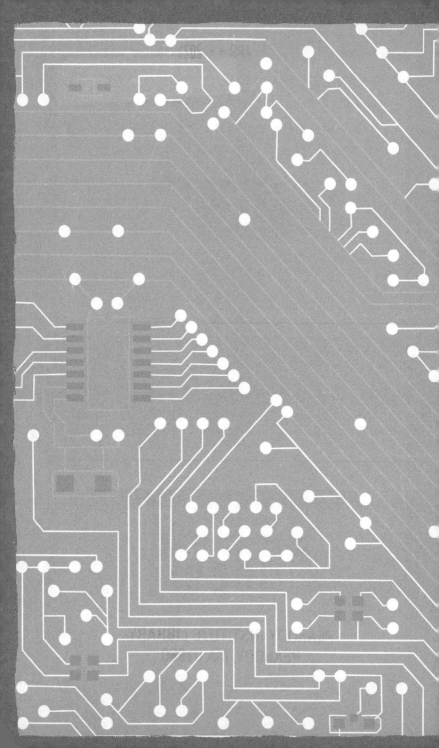

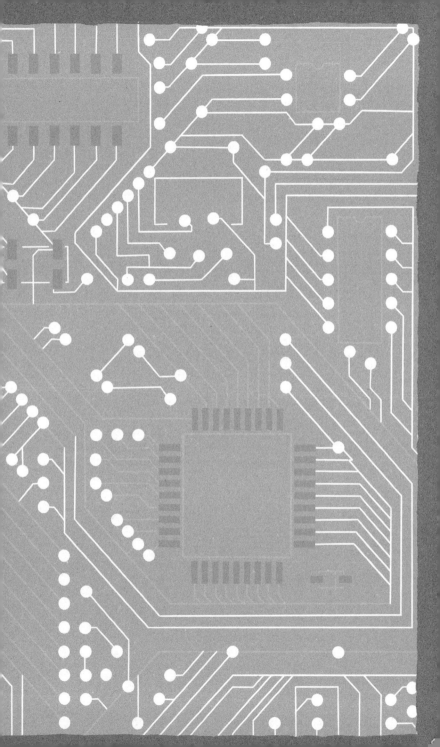

First American Edition 2020
Kane Miller, A Division of EDC Publishing

Original edition first published by Penguin Books Ltd, London
Text copyright © Craig Barr-Green, 2020
Illustrations copyright © Salini Perera, 2020
The author and the illustrator have asserted their moral rights.

For information contact:
Kane Miller, A Division of EDC Publishing
P.O. Box 470663
Tulsa, OK 74147-0663
www.kanemiller.com
www.usbornebooksandmore.com

Library of Congress Control Number: 2020937592

Printed and bound in the United States of America
1 2 3 4 5 6 7 8 9 10
ISBN: 978-1-68464-200-7

THE EXTRAORDINARY LIFE OF

STEVE
JOBS

Written by Craig Barr-Green
Illustrated by Salini Perera

Kane Miller
A DIVISION OF EDC PUBLISHING

WHO WAS
Steve Jobs?

Steve Jobs

was an incredible businessman and inventor who
loved computers. Thanks to his awesome mind,
every smartphone, tablet, laptop, and computer
in the world contains a little bit of Steve's magic.
By the end of his life Steve had changed the
computer, music, movie, and phone industries.

When he was a kid, Steve watched his dad fixing things and learned how to take things apart and **rebuild and repair** them. But Steve's real love was electronics and technology. He was in just the right place at the right time to see his hobby turn into a passion that would change his life . . . and the world.

DID YOU KNOW?

Many people now think that Steve had dyslexia – a common learning difficulty that can cause problems with reading, writing, and spelling. He certainly struggled at, and was often frustrated with, school and studying.

As a young man, alongside his friend Steve Wozniak, Steve started a company called *Apple*, which invented computers that were extremely powerful and popular.

Later, Tim Berners-Lee invented the *World Wide Web* (the internet) on a machine made by Steve Jobs.

Can you imagine life without the internet?

Steve also helped change the way cartoons were made by using brilliant technology. He ran a company called *Pixar* – and their first film was *Toy Story*.

In 2001, Steve gave the world the *iPod*, a device that could hold **a thousand songs** at once. But what came next was something the world had never seen before.

" AN IPOD.
A phone
AND AN INTERNET
communicator."

The iPhone. On one small machine people could now make calls, go online, play games, and message friends — all on the move.

Over 1.5 billion iPhones have been sold to date and the iPhone has transformed the way people play, work, talk, and communicate all over the world.

In 2011, Steve died at age fifty-six after suffering from a tumor. He had achieved so much in so little time as an inventor, a leader, an artist, and a tough businessman. And it all began in 1955.

In San Francisco, California, on February 24, 1955, a baby was put up for **ADOPTION** the moment he was born. Before long, a nice loving couple was found.

ADOPTION: when a baby is born, and their biological parent or parents find someone else to raise them.

But the couple who were due to adopt Steve changed their mind at the very last minute. The next couple on the waiting list got a call in the night and were told about the baby boy. Did the couple want him?

Of course they said yes!

Steve's birth mother made his new parents, Paul and Clara Jobs, sign a document that made them promise to *send the child to* COLLEGE. That was a promise they kept. But little did they know that Steve would eventually drop out of college!

Steven Paul Jobs was completely adored by his kind parents. Paul and Clara weren't able to have children of their own and had long wanted to bring up a baby.

When Steve found out he was adopted he didn't mind at all. Paul and Clara were everything to him. They made sure Steve knew that they had **chosen him** and that they thought he was special. And they were right.

DID YOU KNOW?

In 1957 Paul and Clara adopted another baby: a girl called Patty, who became Steve's little sister.

*P*aul Jobs repaired cars and sold them. He was brilliant at building and fixing things, and the young Steve was amazed by it. Their house had a workbench on which Steve's dad would do all sorts of **handiwork**. Steve learned very early in life that if a job needed to be done, then it should be done well. And if something was being built, even the parts that couldn't be seen should be well made and look right.

At school, Steve became *easily bored* if he didn't find the work challenging. On top of that he liked to play *pranks*. He was SUSPENDED a few times and his parents were sure it was because the teachers weren't making school interesting enough for their son.

SUSPENSION: taking a student out of school temporarily when they've done something wrong.

As he grew older school started to become miserable. Steve was often alone and was sometimes bullied. He *begged* to change schools. And in 1967 the Jobses moved to a new house on Crist Drive in Los Altos, California. The area was full of families that worked in electronics, engineering, and technology.

Los Altos is in the north of what is now known as SILICON VALLEY, and the house on Crist Drive would later become legendary.

SILICON VALLEY:
an area in California famous for its technology and wealth.

Meeting Wozniak

In his teens, Steve made friends with another boy called Steve, though **Steve Wozniak** was known as "Woz." Steve and Woz would fall out from time to time, but they stayed in touch for all Steve Jobs's life.

Steve Wozniak

Woz was brilliant at **electronics**. He was a few years older than Steve. He was an honest, cheerful young man, who liked nothing better than inventing and playing with electronics.

In 1971 and 1972 Steve and Wozniak made a clever (and illegal!) device called a **blue box**. It tricked phone computers into letting them make long-distance calls for free. They even sold a few. This was their first adventure as a double act, but it would not be their last . . .

DID YOU KNOW?

Using their blue box, Steve and Wozniak made one particularly memorable prank phone call. Wozniak dialed the Vatican in Italy and pretended to be a famous American politician called Henry Kissinger. He asked to speak to the Pope! Although, since it was the middle of the night in Italy, the Pope was asleep and the prank didn't quite work as well as he'd hoped.

Reed College

PORTLAND

USA

OREGON

Paul and Clara had promised Steve's birth mother that Steve would go to college, and in 1973 Steve chose **Reed College** in Portland, Oregon. It was very expensive, but his parents managed to scrape together enough money to send him there.

Unfortunately, Steve and college just didn't mix. He was very bright, but he wanted to study what interested him, rather than follow set classes. Steve discovered COUNTERCULTURE, and started reading magazines and attending talks that suggested different ways of looking at life and the universe. He got into music and went to parties and started meeting other people who also believed that there was *more to life* than studying and working.

COUNTERCULTURE: not following the rules expected of you.

Eventually he dropped out of college, but he managed to come to an agreement that he would still attend the classes that interested him. There was one class in particular that blew his mind and changed the way people use computers to this day.

Calligraphy

*A*s soon as he came across it, Steve *fell in love* with calligraphy. The classes were taught by a professor named Robert Palladino. Steve was hooked.

Later he poured his love for calligraphy into his first computers. For the first time people could choose exactly how their words looked on the screen.

Calligraphy is the art of beautiful hand lettering, where letters can be designed and painted or inked in countless ways.

Fonts

When you use a computer to write something you can affect how it looks by choosing a font. The font you are reading now is Officina Sans Std. Early fonts were named after cities that Steve loved. You can't use it now, but his early computers used a font called Chicago.

By changing the letters we can change the look, mood and feel of the writing. Look at the difference between:

this

THIS

this

I changed these fonts very easily on my Mac. I even played with their sizes. Thank you, Steve Jobs! Your great idea has now been used in a book all about you. Isn't that amazing?

Atari

After dropping out of college, Steve got a job working for a computer company called **Atari**. They were famous for one of the first-ever video games, called Pong. It was like table tennis. It looks very *old-fashioned* now, but it is still fun to play!

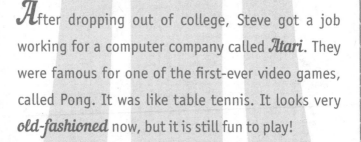

Steve should have been right at home in such a relaxed and clever company. But before long people started to **complain** about him, saying that he was rude to his coworkers. At the time he believed that he didn't need to take showers because he only ate fruit. Several people complained that he stank!

Although Steve was great at his job, people found him such hard work that he was put on the **night shift**. But it didn't bother him. Wozniak, who was working at Hewlett-Packard (a software company) during the day, would come and hang out with Steve on his shifts.

One day Atari set the team the challenge of solving a problem that was bugging a game called *Breakout*, where the player controls a bat while a ball bounces around the screen destroying bricks. Steve said that he could fix it. But instead of doing it himself, he gave the challenge to Woz and offered to split the fee. Wozniak solved the problem in such a complicated way that his design was too difficult for the company to use right away.

The prize money, believed to be around $5,000, caused an argument between the friends. How it was split remains a mystery, but it could be that Steve wasn't completely fair to Woz!

India and spirituality

DID YOU KNOW?

Things that Steve learned from Zen appeared in Apple products, such as the calmness and the simplicity, and the beauty in the design.

From an early age Steve was deeply SPIRITUAL. Steve studied spiritual ideas from India and Japan, and was interested in *Zen Buddhism*. Zen is about harmony and the space between things, and it can be seen in art like calligraphy, where there is a relationship between the lines and the spaces between them.

In 1974 Steve took a break from Atari and visited *India* to learn more about SPIRITUALITY. But he got very ill early in the trip and was sick for some time. He lost an awful lot of weight.

SPIRITUALITY: thinking deeply about life, the world, and the universe, and seeking peace.

When Steve arrived back home his parents didn't recognize him at the airport. In spite of his illness Steve loved what he had seen and learned in India.

Around this time one of Steve's old college friends, Robert Friedland, had taken over an apple farm in Portland, Oregon, which is north of Silicon Valley. He named it *All Farm One*. People would go and stay at the farm to talk and rest and think about life's big questions. In return the guests would work in the orchard, then everyone would eat a big vegetarian meal together. This type of place is called a *commune*.

Steve looked after the apples in the orchard, and famously ate a lot of fruit. The apple would later become important to him, of course, in a very different way.

The Homebrew Computer Club

*I*n 1975 Steve's friend Wozniak visited the Homebrew Computer Club, a meeting where people could show off their ideas and inventions. Although Woz was too shy to talk, he learned about making and using a microprocessor: a *tiny* thing that, he thought, could have *huge* consequences for computing. He believed he could build a computer that could stand alone, with everything it needed to work hidden away inside it. In other words: like the computers we see today.

28

Woz went home and amazed Steve by typing letters on a keyboard that made words appear on a screen. After this, Steve started going to Homebrew Club meetings. He showed everyone Wozniak's work with his amazing energy. Woz and Steve made a great partnership.

In 1976 they presented what would become the very first *Apple computer*. But Steve and Woz disagreed about how to go about this. Wozniak loved the computer so much he wanted to give it away for free so that other people who loved computers could use it and play with it. Steve thought otherwise. He believed that the computer should be sold so they could make money and invent more *amazing things*, and crucially he wanted the machine to be used by *everyone*, not just people who already loved computers.

To do that they would need money to set up a business. Wozniak agreed – Steve had a way of convincing people.

The Apple Computer Company

Soon enough Steve and Woz needed a name for their business. Steve was still spending a lot of time at the All Farm One apple orchard, and they decided to call the business *Apple*. It was a strange name for a computer business – they usually had high-tech or serious names. The name really stood out . . . and so did the computer!

Steve thought that the word "apple" was friendly and encouraging at a time when people were wary of computers.

"PLUS IT WOULD GET US AHEAD OF 'Atari' IN THE PHONE BOOK."

Computers at home

At the time, having a computer at home was something most people hadn't even thought about. It was revolutionary to claim that this could change.

FRAGILE

THIS END UP

To raise money for the company Steve sold his car and Wozniak sold his valuable scientific calculator. They asked an INVESTOR, one of Steve's old friends, Ron Wayne, to be part of the company. Ron agreed, and on April 1, 1976, the Apple Computer Company was born.

Steve and Wozniak owned 45% of the company each and Ron 10%. Very soon, however, Ron pulled out. He sold back his share to Steve and Wozniak.

If Ron Wayne had kept his part of the company, his shares would later have been worth billions of dollars.

Apple quickly got its first big order from a store called The Byte Shop. Steve had turned his parents' house and garage into a **workshop** to build the computers and got help from his closest friends. One by one the computers came off the workbench. Steve inspected them and was furious if he spotted any mistakes or sloppy work.

Apple was in business.

*T*he **Apple I** was exciting but a little scruffy. Steve wanted more style and more control over every bit of the machine. He wanted a beautiful case and special power cords. All of this needed a lot of money. An investor called *Mike Markkula* invested heavily in exchange for owning a third of the business. Steve, Wozniak and Mike Markkula signed a deal and *Apple Computer, Inc.* was born.

While Steve worked tirelessly building up interest in their computers, Wozniak worked his magic; he introduced color to computing, which was an amazing breakthrough. In 1977 they unveiled the **Apple II** and it looked like the future.

A new era of home computing had begun, and Apple was leading the race. Over the next sixteen years the Apple II sold nearly *six million machines*. Apple moved out of the family garage and into an office in Cupertino, where they remain to this day.

The Apple logo

The Apple logo as we know it was designed by Rob Janoff in 1977. The first design looked too much like a cherry, so Steve picked the design that had a bite taken out of it. It is one of the most famous logos in the world and is clearly displayed on every Apple product.

There have been lots of theories about the logo, from the story of Adam and Eve, to Isaac Newton and his falling apple, to the poisoned apple that some people think the brilliant codebreaker Alan Turing ate at the end of his life.

Steve was very *argumentative*. If he didn't like something, he would swear and rage in people's faces. This happened to friends, Apple workers, and even waiters and waitresses. But if he liked something, he would dance with glee and say it was *perfect*. There wasn't much in between! Steve believed in being honest and speaking his mind. He cared greatly about the products he was making.

DID YOU KNOW?

Steve's favorite way to talk to people, and to make big decisions, was to take them on a long walk. Sometimes he would go barefoot. Sometimes his walks would begin as arguments and end on friendly terms with a deal being made.

Millionaire

In 1980 Apple went public. This meant that the public could buy tiny bits of the business (shares) and make or lose money depending on how well Apple performed. It went very well, and **Apple Computer, Inc.** was valued at **$1.79 billion dollars**, an extraordinary amount of money! It made lots of people into instant millionaires – including Steve, even though he was just twenty-five years old!

But then things started to stutter. The follow-ups to the Apple II didn't do as well as Steve had hoped. The **Apple III** launched in 1980 and the **Apple Lisa** in 1983. Both were disappointments. Luckily the Apple II was still selling well.

The Apple Lisa

The Apple Lisa was a curious name. Officially it stood for Locally Integrated Software Architecture. But there was a deeper story. When Steve was young he had had a girlfriend called Chrisann Brennan, who had a baby. Steve said that the baby was not his, despite medical evidence. In 1978 the baby was born on All Farm One. He helped choose the name: Lisa. Steve later admitted Lisa was his daughter and her surname became Brennan-Jobs. The relationship would always be rocky, and Steve regretted his behavior in those early days.

The Apple Macintosh

Apple was growing bigger, and this meant that Steve had even more people to wrestle with to get his own way. One day Steve spotted a small project being researched by an employee called Jef Raskin – a computer that was quite cheap and incredibly simple to use. It would have everything it needed to work all in one package. It wouldn't be the biggest, or the most powerful, computer ever made, but it would be the most straightforward and could be bought and used by anyone. It became known as the *Apple Macintosh*, named after Jef Raskin's favorite type of apple. In the end, to keep the peace, the company decided Steve, who had been kicked off the Apple Lisa project, should take over, and Raskin eventually quit.

Steve began to assemble a brilliant team. He had his own premises in a different part of the Apple offices called Texaco Towers. The team began to think of themselves as *pirates*: doing things their way, led by the fearsome Captain Steve Jobs. He pushed hard for every tiny element to be better, faster, or more beautiful.

The Macintosh gang were in turns exhausted and energized by Steve's nonstop quest for elegant design. Even the parts the customer would never see, deep inside the computer, had to be perfect. Steve remembered what his father had taught him.

In 1979 Steve was invited to visit another computer company called Xerox. They had invested in Apple and allowed Steve to look around their research area. They showed Steve an idea called a graphical user interface (GUI). Instead of looking at a black screen with writing, the user could look at something that was like a desktop with squares (icons) representing the computer's applications (the things it could do). Steve loved it so much he took the idea for himself, and applied its brilliance to a similar project that Apple was reportedly working on. Xerox wasn't happy, but there was nothing they could do.

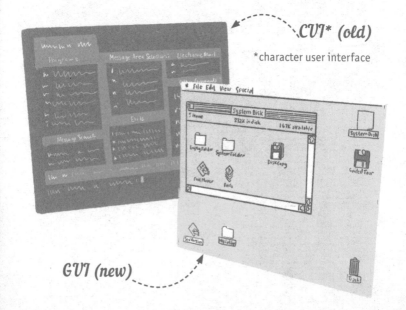

CUI* (old)

*character user interface

GUI (new)

Steve Jobs was a wonderful talker. When he spoke, people listened, whether he was being nice or angry. He hated notes or prepared presentations when he spoke to his staff in meetings and instead would talk and write his ideas up on a whiteboard like a teacher. In the same way, when people needed to explain or report things to him, he would often stop them if they were boring him, or if he thought their ideas weren't any good. On stage he was like a showman, and his product launches became legendary. They became known as **Stevenotes**.

The launch of the Macintosh was the first to truly show Steve's skills. He stood on stage in a smart suit, with the Macintosh hidden inside a bag on a table on the other side of the stage. Steve whipped the crowd into a state of pure **excitement**. Then he showed them the Mac itself, to audible gasps from the audience. It looked unlike anything they had ever seen. Steve started using the computer. He put in a disk and started a demonstration. There were pictures of fonts, games of chess, a painting of Steve Jobs himself, a calculator — business and pleasure all one after the other. The whole act went **perfectly**. The best, though, was yet to come. Steve introduced the Macintosh itself. The audience was silent.

Then the computer spoke.

"HELLO, I'M *Macintosh*. IT SURE IS GREAT TO GET OUT OF THAT BAG."

This was staggering. The computer had made its own speech. It had even made a joke. The crowd gasped and cheered. The *future* was right there on stage and anybody could buy it.

This set the tone for how Apple would launch its greatest products. These weren't simply new bits of technology: these were thrilling, joyous, beautifully designed pieces of art. Steve Jobs molded together his team's ***brilliant minds*** and unveiled things that people hadn't realized they wanted.

Steve created superfans. In the future, people would line up all night outside Apple Stores in order to get their hands on the newest products, no matter what the price. Steve had started a revolution and his fans were his army.

Leaving Apple

Even though Steve was now a star, things were getting rocky for him at Apple. He was often rude to and upset people he considered inferior in talent or intelligence.

Apple was a huge company and was run (like all big companies) by a group of important people called a *board.* They made sure that the company was being run properly and settled any arguments. There were shareholders to think about: all those people who had bought little bits of Apple and made Steve a millionaire. A *CEO* (chief executive officer) was the most senior job. This role was not held by Steve. It was a role that needed great patience and people skills. At that point in his life, Steve might not have been very good at it.

The CEO of Apple was *John Sculley*. Steve had chosen him personally. However, despite a wonderful start to their relationship, things began to go wrong quite rapidly.

Steve and the board had very different ideas about what Apple should be doing. In the end it became a power struggle between the two men. Steve turned on John. Some of the board backed Steve and some backed John. In 1985 Steve left the company that he had co-created. He felt he had no other option. He no longer felt welcome.

NeXT

Steve convinced some of his favorite Apple staff to leave with him to create a new project: *NeXT*. This was a computer that would be used in businesses, colleges and universities. It was a different direction for Steve.

The computer was a cube, which meant that, although it looked futuristic, building it was extremely tricky. It came with a new operating system called NeXTSTEP. An operating system controls what a computer does, so it is incredibly important. NeXTSTEP was exciting to the computing world.

The NeXT paved the way for **electronic books** (e-books). After making a deal with *Oxford University Press*, the NeXT would come packaged with the complete works of Shakespeare and the *Oxford Dictionary of Quotations*. On top of that, they included a thesaurus and a complete dictionary. These books were searchable and helped create a way for books to be read electronically — something that is common now.

But the machine was delayed. Steve *created his own factory* to build the NeXTs and, as always, it had to look perfect and operate beautifully. Everything was costing more than expected and Steve was running out of money.

Steve was certain that everything would go to plan and he demanded more from his team. He had what some people called a *"reality distortion field."* This meant that he could change what people thought was possible. By the sheer force of his personality, he could make people do things they thought were impossible. It worked with the Apple Macintosh, but at NeXT it caused delays.

The NeXT finally launched on October 12, 1988. It was another *spectacular* event. Steve was on stage for three hours and spoke with enormous energy about the amazing features and the game-changing software. A violinist even came on stage and played a duet with the computer!

Unfortunately, because the machine had cost so much to make and still wasn't completely finished, the price was a staggering $6,500. This was so much more than most people expected or could even afford.

It had **disappointing sales**, despite how good it was. Although it didn't change the world in the way he expected, his ideas certainly didn't go to waste. People had learned to expect the unexpected with Steve, and his next adventure took him:

DID YOU KNOW?
Sir Tim Berners-Lee invented the World Wide Web on a NeXT computer. He found the computer and software incredibly easy to use.

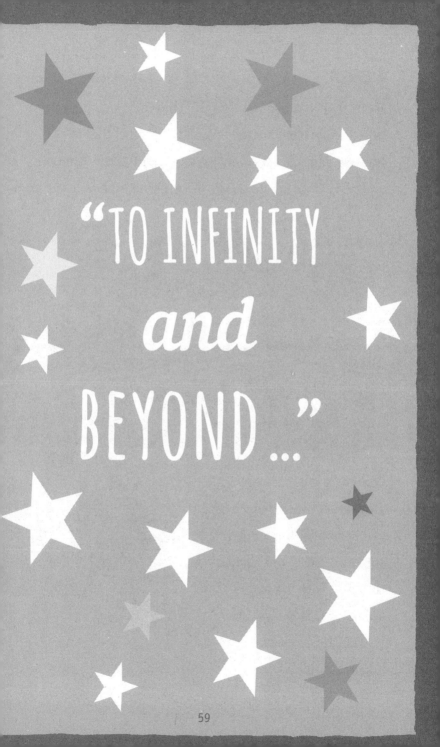

"TO INFINITY *and* BEYOND..."

Pixar

Steve always worked on lots of things at once. Back in 1985 he had been invited to look at a project that might surprise him. Off he went to the **Skywalker Ranch** owned by **George Lucas**, the man behind **Star Wars**.

George ran a company called **Lucasfilm**, which had a small team that made computers and software that did incredible things with images and animation. Steve was stunned. It was the perfect mix of art and technology.

In 1986 he agreed to buy the little company, called the Graphics Group, and become its chairman. At the heart of the company was the *Pixar Image Computer*. Steve renamed the company after this machine: *Pixar*. His plan was to sell this computer to organizations that needed to use complicated images. Although the computers were amazing, they cost $125,000 and very few were sold.

A cheaper model was issued, but it still cost $30,000!

P·I·X·A·R

Pixar found ways of making animation easier. They were so good at it that *Disney* began using a Pixar package to help make their movies.

Steve became mesmerized by the work of John Lasseter, who ran the animation division. To show off the brilliance of Pixar technology to customers, Lasseter made a cartoon called *Luxo Jr.* He based the main character on the *lamp* he kept on his desk. The short film told the story of a lamp playing ball with a younger, smaller lamp. It was so warm and funny that it received a nomination for an Academy Award.

ACADEMY AWARDS: prizes given out each year to the very best films and the people that made them and starred in them. They are also known as the Oscars.

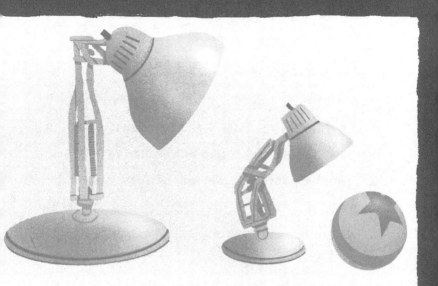

Luxo Jr. and Ball became the
Pixar mascots. You can see
them at the start of every
Pixar movie. Pixar's next
short animated film was
called *Tin Toy*, and that
actually won an Academy
Award. The idea of a movie
based on a gang of toys caught

the attention of Disney. Soon enough Pixar and Disney
agreed to make movies together. This relationship would
prove to be a very fiery one. Nevertheless, in 1995 the
full-length movie *Toy Story* was released and was a
smash hit, changing animation and cinema forever.

Billionaire

Steve and Disney argued a lot. Pixar may have made *Toy Story*, but Disney released it and had their name on it. They had an agreement to make three films together, but Steve wanted more. He wanted Pixar's name on the movie as well. Disney disagreed. But winning arguments was something that Steve Jobs was very good at!

To begin with, in order to raise money, he did what he had done at Apple and made Pixar public, which meant that people could buy shares. He thought it would go well, but it went far better than he could have dreamed.

On November 29, 1995, the shares that Steve had bought for $5 million were now worth $1.2 billion. Steve was a *billionaire*. He finally reached a new fifty-fifty agreement with Disney. Pixar now had its name on the movies alongside Disney.

Pixar became as big a brand as Apple. Steve really did have the magic touch. Even though he took over the company to sell computers (and failed!) he had seen the potential for animated movies.

Pixar made hit after hit. Here are the first ten films they made. Each film won an Academy Award. How many have you seen?

Toy Story (1995)
A Bug's Life (1998)
Toy Story 2 (1999)
Monsters, Inc. (2001)
Finding Nemo (2003)
The Incredibles (2004)
Cars (2006)
Ratatouille (2007)
Wall-E (2008)
Up (2009)

Finding his family

Steve had always thought the world of Paul and Clara Jobs. He had always known that he had been adopted, but not the full details.

Clara Jobs died in 1986. Steve spent lots of time with her before she died and she told him more about his adoption.

A few years earlier he had contacted the doctor whose name was on his **birth certificate**. The doctor said that the details of his birth had been lost in a fire, but this wasn't true. Instead of telling Steve the truth over the phone, he wrote down some details about Steve's birth mom in a letter. He insisted that it could only be sent to him after the doctor's death. That's exactly what happened. When the doctor died the letter was sent.

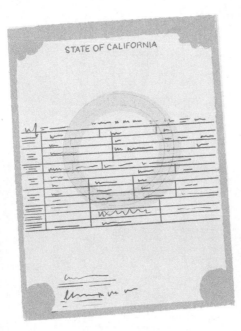

After Clara's death Steve asked his dad, Paul, whether he was allowed to try to find his birth mom. Paul agreed. When Steve finally found his birth mom, Joanne, she filled in the gaps in his life story. She had married his birth father, Abdulfattah, and had another baby, a girl called *Mona*. Steve had a biological sister he knew nothing about! He learned that Joanne and Abdulfattah had split up and that she and Mona didn't see much of him.

Joanne

Mona

Joanne finally learned about Steve's **_extraordinary life_**. She was very proud and very sorry for putting him up for adoption. Steve was simply grateful that he had been born and had been able to live his life. They became close for the first time in their lives.

Steve eventually met his biological sister when he was twenty-seven and she was twenty-five. The two became great friends, although they were a little nervous at first. Mona was an author living in New York.

Abdulfattah

Steve never knowingly met his birth father. With Steve's help, Mona tracked him down, but Steve asked her not to reveal to their father who he was. Mona learned that her father had moved around a lot. He told her that he had owned restaurants. There was one that was popular with rich people working in technology. In fact, even Steve had visited! Mona was shocked. Abdulfattah **didn't know** that Steve was his son. Mona kept Steve's identity a secret.

Mona told the story to Steve and he was stunned. He remembered the restaurant! Later on, when Abdulfattah finally discovered the truth, the two still didn't want to meet . . . and never did.

Falling in love

In 1989 Steve met a woman called Laurene Powell. She was sitting in the front row of a lecture he was giving and afterward they went out for a meal together. Laurene was funny, strong, and intelligent, and for Steve it was love at first sight. She was tough enough to handle his moods!

Two years later, on March 18, 1991, Steve and Laurene got **married**. They had a spiritual wedding at Yosemite National Park. It was snowing hard. Steve and Laurene stayed together for the rest of Steve's life. Together they had three children: Reed, Erin, and Eve. And over the years he worked hard to make things better between him and his first daughter, Lisa.

Back at Apple

In Steve's absence things were not going well back at Apple. The answer to their problem was . . . NeXT. All the amazing things Steve and his team had designed at NeXT were exactly what Apple needed. So Apple bought the company. In 1997, twelve years after leaving, Steve was back at the company he had co-created.

A buzz of excitement swept through Apple and the world of technology. Things moved quickly. Steve had some power. He moved from adviser to temporary CEO and then, in 2000, he became the official boss. He was running Apple.

Things were about to become very exciting indeed.

The Steve Jobs uniform

Steve had a very distinctive look. He didn't wear a suit and tie like most businesspeople. He asked the Japanese fashion designer Issey Miyake to make him a black turtleneck sweater. In fact, he ordered a lifetime's worth! He often wore Levi's jeans and New Balance sneakers. Even though he was a rich, successful businessman, he still wanted to be "counterculture." So just as teenage Steve had had long hair, ripped jeans, and walked barefoot, the older Steve Jobs very much had his own look. With his shaved head, stubbly beard, and round glasses, Steve was instantly recognizable.

black
turtleneck
sweater

Levi's
jeans

New
Balance
sneakers

The iPod and the iTunes Store

*I*n 2001 Steve showed the *iPod* to the world. In one of his most famous launches he stood on the stage with no props. He reached into his pocket and pulled out a small machine. This was the iPod. It allowed the user to carry 1,000 songs and had a wheel that let you dial through your songs. It was *simple*. It was *powerful*. It looked like the *future*. Before this people carried bulky portable CD or cassette players. The iPod instantly made everything else out of date.

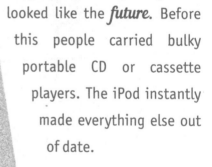

Steve Jobs was a huge music fan, so this was something he built as much for himself as for the public. For the first time people could "shuffle" their music, a feature that randomly picked the song to be played next.

Steve was changing the music industry. *iTunes* followed
– software that helped people organize music on their
computers. And Apple was in control of the whole
process. They had the computer, the software and the
iPod. Other companies could only stand and stare in
amazement.

To stop people committing MUSIC PIRACY Steve made
deals with record labels. They were unsure at first, but
trusted in his big ideas and the amazing iPod.

MUSIC PIRACY:
when people take
music files for free
from the internet.

In 2006 a man called Alex Ostrovsky bought the billionth song from the store. He won an iMac, ten iPods, and a $10,000 gift card.

In 2003 the iTunes Store sold twenty-five million songs. The iPod soon became available in different shapes and sizes, including ones that showed videos, and one that had no screen and only shuffled songs. Once again Steve Jobs knew what we wanted before we knew ourselves.

Steve could spot talent and he struck gold again when he met the English designer *Jony Ive*. Jony was so talented Steve trusted him and promoted him quickly, which was rare! Jony helped design all of Apple's greatest products, including the iPod, right up to 2019. He is regarded as one of the world's greatest designers.

Nelson Mandela

Gandhi

Amelia Earhart

In 1997 a huge campaign called **Think Different** was launched. The TV commercial was originally narrated by Steve. It started with the words "Here's to the crazy ones." It was followed by black-and-white images of extraordinary people who had led extraordinary lives. The list included people like Gandhi (the peace activist), Albert Einstein (the physicist), Maria Callas (the opera singer), John Lennon (the rock star), Alfred Hitchcock (the film director), and Amelia Earhart (the pilot). Despite being an expensive advertisement to sell Apple products, the commercial didn't show a single one. Now that IS thinking differently!

John Lennon

Muhammad Ali

Albert Einstein

iPhone

What was better than an iPod? The answer: an iPod that was also a phone. On June 29, 2007, Apple released the *iPhone* and it caused a *sensation*. It was a phone that had an iPod inside it, as well as a camera, an internet browser, calendars, emails, messages, a video player, games, a compass, reminders . . . everything in one place, in your hand. It had a glass touchscreen that could be easily used with just your finger. Who needed buttons? The screen could change from a phone to a keyboard to a video screen just like that. It was stylish and incredibly easy to use straight out of the box (which itself was designed beautifully by Jony and Steve Jobs).

Mobile phones already existed, but Steve felt that the public rarely used many of the phones' features because they were too *complicated*. This invention sent shock waves around the world. The technology might have existed elsewhere, but the iPhone made it easy and effortless and, as Steve himself would often say, "insanely great."

Steve and Wozniak had written inside their old blue box, "He's got the whole world in his hands." Now, more than ever, Steve Jobs had made these words feel true. Later Apple would introduce the iCloud, which allowed all Apple devices to connect to each other without wires. Now people were more *connected* to everyone and everything than ever before. This was Steve's love of Zen in action.

Apps

Have you ever played a game on a phone or a tablet? Crushing candy, helping chickens across roads, firing at birds with a catapult, surfing subways or building cities out of blocks? Games are just one example of an "app." Apps have always existed in computing, but now they are more popular and easier to use than ever before. They can be used for absolutely anything: from looking up train times, using Facebook and Twitter, watching YouTube, and calling a ride, to doing your shopping, reading a newspaper, and even helping doctors and surgeons.

In 2008 the App Store was released. All the available apps were grouped by category and popularity, and it was an instant success. Sales went through the roof again.

The iPad

In January 2010 the *iPad* was released. It was a thin, beautiful touchscreen tablet that was the middle point between an iPhone and a laptop computer.

It was so simple it didn't need a manual. You just needed a finger to use it. The iPad's larger screen meant that app designers could be even more adventurous. In the eighteen months following the iPad's release, the App Store had an incredible *425,000* apps.

In 2011 Apple became the most valuable company in the world. Steve Jobs was on a roll.

Apple sold a *million* iPads in the first month.

Illness

Although Apple was in the best health of its life, Steve Jobs had been battling a terrible illness. And he was exhausted, juggling Apple and Pixar, and working hard.

In October 2003, Steve was diagnosed with **PANCREATIC CANCER**. It made him very ill. He must have been in lots of pain, but Steve surprised people by choosing not to have traditional *medical treatment*.

PANCREAS: part of the body used for digestion. It sits in the upper part of the abdomen, behind the stomach.

However, in 2004, he had surgery after all. He became very thin and allowed others at Apple to do parts of his job. His health became worse over the years, and in 2009 he had a liver transplant. It was a *success* and he went back to work.

"YOUR TIME IS LIMITED, SO DON'T WASTE IT LIVING *someone else's life . . .* DON'T LET THE NOISE OF OTHERS' OPINIONS DROWN OUT YOUR OWN INNER VOICE. AND MOST IMPORTANT, HAVE THE COURAGE TO FOLLOW YOUR *heart and intuition.*"

A year and a half after going back to work, however, he decided to take some time off. On August 24, 2011, he announced his resignation as CEO of Apple.

He stayed on as a chairman of the board, but he died six weeks later, on October 5, at the age of fifty-six. He was at home, surrounded by his wife and children and his two sisters.

After looking at them all his final words were:

"OH WOW.
Oh wow.
OH WOW."

Living in a Steve Jobs world

Steve Jobs had instinct. He made his own products that did things his way. He surrounded himself with the very best minds and he got the very best out of them. He had a feel for what the future might look like, and he designed products to take us there. People had no idea that the thing they needed most was a computer with a desktop, or a thousand songs in their pockets, or a mobile phone that contained the internet and their music. Even his Apple Stores were futuristic, including the *floating glass staircases* that he helped design.

DID YOU KNOW?

A person or company can claim an idea as their own by receiving a patent. Steve Jobs is credited as having 458 patents – a third being credited after his death!

Steve is listed as a designer of the amazing glass cube store that can be found on 5th Avenue in New York City.

99

From the very beginning Steve was a man with deep ideas and dreams. He drove people up the wall, but delighted millions. He was a perfectionist; he didn't like being told what to do and learned best by finding out things for himself. He could be charming when he wanted, and some people did their best work with him. He was an artist, a hard businessman, and a spiritual soul. All of these things combined to make Steve Jobs extraordinary.

What was his secret? This is what young Steve Jobs had to say:

"LIFE CAN BE MUCH BROADER

once you discover

ONE SIMPLE FACT

and that is everything around you that you call

LIFE

was made up by people that were no smarter

THAN YOU.

"AND YOU CAN CHANGE IT. YOU CAN INFLUENCE IT . . . YOU CAN BUILD YOUR OWN THINGS THAT OTHER PEOPLE CAN USE . . . ONCE YOU LEARN THAT YOU WILL NEVER BE THE SAME AGAIN."

Steve liked to end every one of his launches by saying a catchphrase that guaranteed he had the final word. Before revealing an amazing final piece of information he would say . . .

?

February 24, 1955

Steve is born in San Francisco and adopted by Paul and Clara Jobs.

1967

The family moves to Crist Drive, Los Altos, near Silicon Valley.

1973

Steve goes to Reed College, but drops out. He stays on to attend classes that interest him.

Steve discovers Zen Buddhism and counterculture.

1977

Mike Markkula invests in Apple.
Rob Janoff designs the famous
Apple logo.

1976

Steve and Wozniak show off an
early Apple I at the Homebrew
Computer Club.

Steve, Wozniak, and Ron Wayne
set up the Apple Computer
Company, before Ron Wayne
pulls out.

They start selling Apple I
computers from the Jobses'
family garage.

1974

Steve works for Atari and
engages Wozniak to solve
the *Breakout* problem.

He takes a break to
explore India.

1978

The Apple II launches.

Lisa Brennan is born. Steve denies being her father, but later admits that he is.

1980

Apple goes public and Steve becomes a millionaire.

1984

The Apple Macintosh is unveiled at a spectacular launch.

hello.

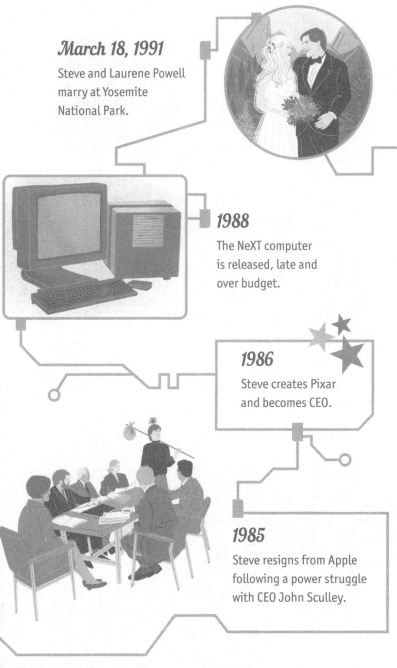

March 18, 1991
Steve and Laurene Powell marry at Yosemite National Park.

1988
The NeXT computer is released, late and over budget.

1986
Steve creates Pixar and becomes CEO.

1985
Steve resigns from Apple following a power struggle with CEO John Sculley.

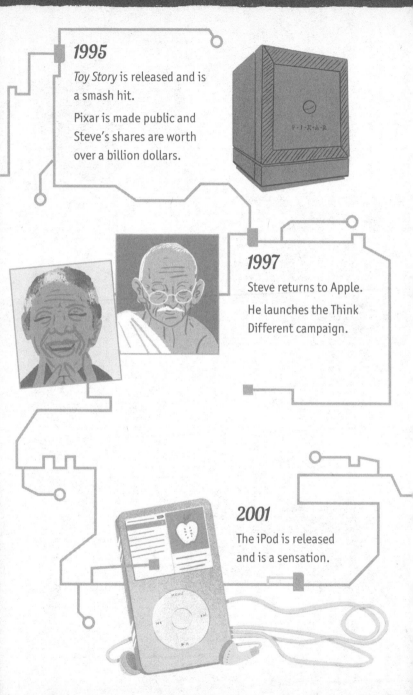

1995

Toy Story is released and is a smash hit.

Pixar is made public and Steve's shares are worth over a billion dollars.

1997

Steve returns to Apple.

He launches the Think Different campaign.

2001

The iPod is released and is a sensation.

October 5, 2011

Steve dies, age fifty-six.

2010

The iPad is released.

2007

Steve launches the iPhone.

2003

Steve is diagnosed with pancreatic cancer.

More about Silicon Valley

"I FEEL INCREDIBLY LUCKY TO BE AT EXACTLY THE RIGHT PLACE IN SILICON VALLEY, AT EXACTLY THE RIGHT TIME, HISTORICALLY, WHERE THIS INVENTION HAS TAKEN FORM."

Silicon Valley is in the southern part of the San Francisco Bay area in the Santa Clara Valley.

Have a look at these maps.

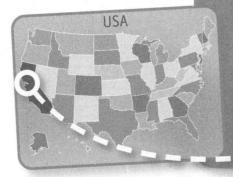

USA

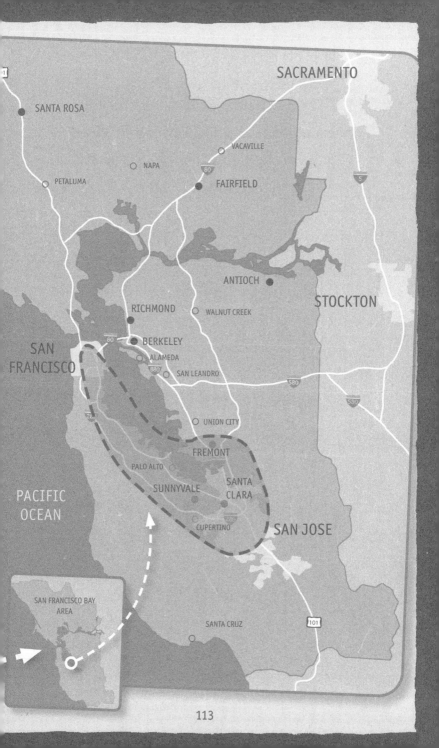

The Santa Clara Valley includes cities like Mountain View, Los Altos, Cupertino, and Palo Alto. All of these areas played an important part in Steve Jobs's life.

Before technology took over it was known as the Valley of Heart's Delight because of the rolling orchards full of fruit. It became known for its technology and engineering research. Late in life, when Steve was helping to design the enormous Apple headquarters in Cupertino, he insisted on including lots of pretty apricot orchards.

Silicon is the second-most abundant element on Earth and the seventh in the universe. Engineers realized that silicon worked amazingly well in semiconductors. Think of them as building blocks for technology.

^{14}
Si
silicon

Semiconductors can be found everywhere: in your computers, mobile phones, and gaming machines. People are constantly looking for new ways to make their technology faster and more powerful than ever before. Not only is this rapidly changing the way we live and work, it's also *very* big business!

Back in 1971 a journalist called Don Hoefler made the term Silicon Valley popular by using it in an article for *Electronic News*. Lots of people claim to have used it first, or invented it, but it was Hoefler who brought it to everyone's attention.

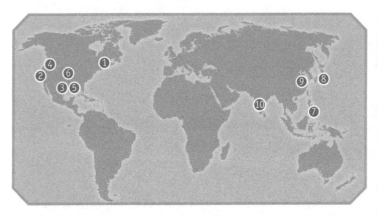

In America alone there is: Silicon Alley, New York City, New York (1); Silicon Beach, Los Angeles, California (2); Silicon Hills, Austin, Texas (3); Silicon Forest, Portland, Oregon (4); Silicon Prairie, Dallas, Texas (5); and Silicon Slopes, Salt Lake City, Utah (6). In Asia there is: Silicon Gulf in the Philippines (7); Silicon Island in Japan (8); Silicon Peninsula in China (9); and Silicon Plateau in India (10).

Some things to think about

Start looking around you when you are in a cafe or on a bus or the train or even in your living room.

Can you spot an iPhone? Is anyone using an iPad? Can you see any Apple logos? You'll start noticing Apple products *everywhere*. Even this book was written on an Apple Macbook.

Steve Jobs was a very passionate leader. What do you think are the key parts of his personality that made him a good leader?

Steve was able to imagine a device
that would completely change the way we live our lives.
Can you imagine a brilliant new device of your own?

Index

Quote Sources

Direct quotes throughout are taken from the following sources:

Page 4: Steve Jobs: iPhone launch, 2007. https://www.youtube.com/watch?v=GK55ElsVzxM

Page 33: Walter Isaacson, *Steve Jobs* (Little, Brown, 2011)

Page 49: The Lost 1984 Video: young Steve Jobs introduces the Macintosh. https://www.youtube.com/watch?v=2B-XwPjn9YY

Page 59: *Toy Story* (Walt Disney Pictures, 1995)

Page 97: Sam Jones, "Steve Jobs's last words: 'Oh wow. Oh wow. Oh wow.'" (Guardian, October 2011)

Pages 102–103: Steve Jobs: iChanged the World (Pioneer Productions for Channel 4, 2011)

Page 105: One More Thing.... https://www.youtube.com/watch?v=hvlHi7iTdaw

Page 112: Steve Jobs: The Lost Interview, dir. by Paul Sen (Magnolia Home Entertainment, 2012)

Have you read about all of these extraordinary people?

Galaxi

"You will meet your god in the present moment," Cathryn Hankla writes, and her poems, emanating from that promise, contemplate and honor the largest questions. The multiverse of this quietly mind-blowing book is composed of imagined constellations— the Labyrinth Galaxy, Some Assembly Required Galaxy, Galaxy Without a Hammer, Lonely Horse Galaxy, and more. The timeframe expands from antiquity to the present; the diurnal braids with the eternal; macro and micro are intertwined. But Hankla also understands the power of fragments—whether archeological or linguistic. She meditates on temporal constructs—*after, when, until*—considers the *where* of *s*pace, and mourns the planet's transience in poems that address creaturely mortality and the loss of ecosystems. The poignancy is sharpened by a devastating irony, for *Galaxies* is a brave book—both canny and infinitely curious. The poems navigate the tangles of family, DNA's braid of connectedness, while giving voice to loneliness, romantic love, and the mysteries of luck. There's a profound delicacy throughout, a candor tempered by compassion. Reticence has seldom seemed so provocative or quietude so dazzling.

    —Alice Fulton, author of *Barely Composed*, MacArthur Fellow

In Cathryn Hankla's *Galaxies,* one cannot escape the influence of the stars. The stars followed lead us often astray into the unexpected, the wonderful, the off-kilter, and the strange. If fate is a road followed, it is full of switchbacks, dangerous curves, washed-out roads, detours, and dead ends. But what a journey Hankla takes us on.

    —Eric Pankey, author of *Crow-Work*

In *Galaxies,* Cathryn Hankla's "orb-struck" book of poems, "language grows like fescue" and the patterns that she creates with it spiral upward from earthbound fact and observation to stellar connections and intuitions. "Too many worlds make up each human," she writes, and her ability to suggest these many worlds, both seen and unseen, "as above and so below," as in a bee colony's "black hole/in a split juniper trunk," result in poems of lyric capaciousness, thoughtful, intricate, and enticing.

    —Carol Moldaw, author of *So Late, So Soon*

The finely crafted poems in Cathryn Hankla's *Galaxies* have a quiet power, a solid emotional core enhanced by playful language that never fails to attract the ear. Both earthy and otherworldly, the poems contained here make lovely leaps of sound and sense, but always return to their task of comprehending the infinite galaxies that hold and define us.

    —Wyn Cooper, author of *Chaos is the New Calm*

Galaxies

Cathryn Hankla

MERCER UNIVERSITY PRESS | *Macon, Georgia*
2017

MUP/ P545

© 2017 Cathryn Hankla
Published by Mercer University Press
1501 Mercer University Drive
Macon, Georgia 31207
All rights reserved

9 8 7 6 5 4 3 2 1

Books published by Mercer University Press are printed on acid-free paper
that meets the requirements of the American National Standard for
Information Sciences—Permanence of Paper for Printed Library Materials.

ISBN   978-0-88146-616-4
Cataloging-in-Publication Data is available from the Library of Congress

Contents

Acknowledgments

The author wishes to thank Colorado Art Ranch, Virginia Center for the Creative Arts, The Jackson Center for Creative Writing at Hollins University, Carol Moldaw, Thorpe Moeckel, and the editors of journals and anthologies in which poems first appeared.

Appalachian Heritage: "Cedar," "Galaxy of the Courthouse Steps."
Cincinnati Review: "90-day Wonder," "The Labyrinth Galaxy," "The Palm Galaxy."
Denver Quarterly: "Conquistadors in the Colonies."
Hampden-Sydney Poetry Review: "Galaxy of Waiting."
La Fovea: "Lizard," "Endtimes:"
Mississippi Review: "Transformations."
Poetry East: "Lonely Horse Galaxy," "Ghost Horses and the Morning Sky."
Pool: "The No Galaxy," "Erased Galaxy."
Shenandoah: "Saving the Earth" (retitled here "Goodbye") "Perihelion, an Elegy for the Neon Man," "Bee Tree."
Shenandoah: 20 years of Poetry: "Bee Tree."
StorySouth: "Invasion," "Erasure," "Slavish Devotion," "Famous Brains."
The Album: "The Ice Convoy."
The Southern Poetry Anthology III: Southern Appalachia: "Bee Tree," "Ghost Horses and the Morning Sky."
Atlas Magazine, World Poetry Portfolio #65: "Some Assembly Required," "Tree of rePent," "Eclipsed," "Galaxy Without a Hammer," "Backward Glance," "The Buffalo Return," "Galaxy of Virginia History," "Not Einstein," "Shakespeare Galaxy," "May Meteors," "One Girl's Discoveries," "Glass Galaxy."
World English Poetry, Sudeep Sen, Ed., Dhaka, Bangladesh: Bengal Publications, 2015: "Some Assembly Required," "Tree of 'rePent,'" "Eclipsed."

galaxy ('gæləksɪ)

1. island universe, from the Greek *galaxias* or "milky"; any of a vast number of systems composed of stars, stellar remnants, gas, dust, and dark matter, held together by gravitational attraction. Galaxies come in a variety of shapes (regular or irregular), sizes, and ages, and most contain black holes at their centers.

2. a splendid gathering, esp. of famous or distinguished people.

The Labyrinth Galaxy

In the Labyrinth Galaxy one is always walking
in what passes for a line. One is possibly moving
along an impossible curve. It is standard
to trace circles and think you are not, as a rock sends water
in concentric waves when hurtled into a pond.
Don't let any of this distract you. The goal
is to be ever in motion toward your god. Keep going,
keep swimming and walking, whether you are to dance hot coals,
slog mud, or troll chest-high sludge. Don't look up unless you stop
altogether. Galay in your gaiters. Don't look down unless
you cough. The goal is to be ever in motion toward your god.
One jump will not do it. You must go around.
The spiral twists open while your eyes are glued shut.
You will meet your god in the present moment,
where the shape disappears, the journey collapses.
The goal is to be ever in motion toward your god.
You will meet your god near the sound of rushing water,
on a picnic bench surrounded by hedges,
as you sit with your legs comfortably crossed.

Migration

Exclamations of snow join
black crows diving

into green fields. On fall nights
language grows like fescue.

Scattered sticks, rustling feet,
cage a-clatter until sky

speaks in tongues of sun.
Down the map

swarming orange and black,
our monarchs left us.

Orion rests on the horizon,
belt slinging up and up and up.

I tilt my head, held fast to earth,
orb struck.

Snowing Fast

Darkness fell as snow quickened. I
skidded, feverish. I wanted to get home. Cars and trucks
halted at the base of Catawba Mountain. Drivers
spelled engines, idling for warmth.

A knock on my window. Black cap and mittens. He
signaled words like fish in a barrel,
eyelids starred with snow, lips cracked like
drumheads of moose, stretched and stained with human oil.

Red lights flashed. He looked nothing like you.
In fact, I no longer thought about our solemn promise. No
one moved or spoke. He turned back to the road, leaving
foggy breath marks and footprints.

With two wrecks ahead, someone made a U. My
penitent car sported worthy tires. I
followed, slurring from Catawba.
Circumnavigating, sliding the darkened country road

wound like a Slinky—lanes indistinguishable
from ebbing shoulders, the moon having fled—I gripped
the wheel and counted on things I could never know
to help me steer, to keep me from vanishing in the snow.

The Palm Galaxy

It's easy to get lost in the leaves,
eyes snaking the entanglement
of what natives call *the fronds*.
At first there's only a small plot of ground
that puts you in mind of a teepee or a simple tent.
You know, you think you know the rest.
The main story's a bit different, a bitmap
for a bit part—then it all starts to shift in a weird
direction. And when it does it's easier to lose bearings
than stand still. You just keep going in the secret
scheme, a game plan. You hope the water's potable,
that someone has at least taken a perc
or a soil sample, some kind of test please,
enough to ease the mind. Where red stakes
balance, earth roils. You mark an X
on your chart. Your plan is just an infant,
a lone, whining cry for a bottle of smeared Milky Way.
But you know that in the Palm Galaxy proper
the sagging length of a green living branch
would shade your troubled head:

There, you wouldn't be alone with your thoughts.
There, you'd wake to the thrum of the tumba.
There, there, there, where the breeze tumbles
the light weave of a living, breathing tree.

Perihelion, an Elegy for the Neon Man

Persephone, I thought you were all to me,
your name crisp as fate,
bright as the bite of an apple.

The man believed in you too, ingénue,
and later perigee, to his spells
cast in gas-filled tubes.
He showed us the glassy reds and blues.
Our eyes squeezed to points in half-light,
basked in examples of electric hues.
He plucked the obsolete blaze of red from a carton,
convinced we could see what he saw, the difference
between a brushfire and the glow of Mars.

Now I trust this leaf, a bit of litter turned to lace, a snowflake
melted by three seasons, eaten by light
and wind and rain,
held on my palm, an omen.

Now I trust these patterns, as above and so below,
the singing underworld,
the point of orbit closest to the earth
that can bring a young man's head, hoisted in the air,
in contact with a cord of a million volts—
that can move a young man's body, or a celestial orb,
to the point in the path nearest to the sun.

Transformations

Once I saw a lizard trying to oust another lizard. A frog swimming backward into a lily pad and a hyacinth flowering tall overhead. My vantage was as dangerous as a rusty nail on the boardwalk. The pond cracked without warning and 911 RESCUE began, in the middle of the night. The truth slipped in...like, like, like...as, as, as... nothing else, no metaphors at all. This is what the truth does and what the truth is.

After the birthday party favors unfurled, water began to seep. The fish, six healthy carp, sank lower and air filled the space they left. What could be done but find the hose? A steady stream interrupted by dreams. Or rather, the opposite: I dreamed and every two hours rose to tramp outside with the flashlight trained on the water level, while yards away the new pond sat idle, not quite dug. I could have shoveled faster, but my uncle died of cancer. Then a drought took out the moon.

And when it was thoroughly out, the moon that is, life began again but was over, somehow, too. As when a fish becomes a frog in the dark of night. As when an uncle dies into the earth, after most of his flesh has drawn away. His skull becomes the moon. A fish floats inside its bowl, swim bladder out of whack, still gulping food.

I could tell you, couldn't I, if you needed to know the truth? Not just any, but *the* truth? I could tell you, couldn't I? Just you? And then you would know.

And that could turn into love, couldn't it?

Some Assembly Required Galaxy

It's not what you imagined, these
late nights of glue and limitation,

hands salt-sticky from snacks,
directions in three dead tongues.

You begin a Braille translation,
parts spread over the shred of rug

not puppy soiled. Setting aside
singular shapes, stacking baggies

of bolts, you time your breaks
to shaggy dog's piddles and poops,

convert to the church of the socket
wrench, metal screw, and wing nut.

Another month or year passes
while you buy the pictured tools,

matching a drill bit from aisle five,
bin three, to black lines sketched

in China. Now the old dog creaks.
You learn to navigate the alp

of stacked parts half awake.
And in the minutes between

dreaming and sleep, you work.
You work until you get it right.

Tree of "rePent"

Painted letters drip red. "P" provides
an awkward sickle tacked to a stalk.
If we found canned peaches for sale

or fresh fuzz from Georgia, if this sign
meant produce or were simply a target
shot ragged, scarred bark shining through,

if fancy jars of quince sealed with wax
and mounds of beefsteak tomatoes awaited us,
if we were offered a modest map of salvation

in an unlikely spot, that would be welcome.
Way past midnight, it won't help to slow down
or speed. Our headlights find the sign

pitch-perfect. The tree of "rePent"
suggests its own necessity as cars slink
home. Tired drivers are not thinking

of or waiting for salvation. LO!—
this handmade inscription on a wooden slab,
admonition that balances a living tree.

Eclipsed

Blinded by a chance at permanence,
via satellite I watch a sliver
of Alaskan sun,
wishing darkness could bloom.

To save your sight,
you follow the disarmed orb
focused through pinholes
or multiplied by leaves.

The lightshow dances
the grass, a primitive projection
so much like a marriage as it ends.
No one can gaze straight at the sun.

Cold echoes into spring
no matter where you are or who.
I drink from this glass alone,
blotted again by the moon.

Galaxy Without a Hammer

Refining these impatient ores/ With hammer and with blaze,/
Until the designated light/ Repudiate the forge.
—Emily Dickinson, "365"

A redheaded woodpecker
works a sycamore upside down,
quinto looking for a conga,
a confutation on a wet October day.

No trail maps . . . only footfalls
left behind. No cigarette butts,
no windy conversation.
The grey fox went missing, tracks

dispersed. The writer who can't
tell maple from oak, knows audience
from witness. The world is no place
to be alone with a dictionary or

a writer. In the wetlands nature study
area: black cherry, poplar, black willow,
tall alder bushes, turtlehead plants
bearing white enfolded heads—

all species tolerant of walnut, which
is dye and food and as toxic
as it tastes. Cyanide
of the forest in green tough hides.

Don't populate my brownies with
bitterness. Iron nutcracker dog's
wide grin crushes fibrous almond shells
with rhythmic tail wags.

In the west, a shelter of reclaimed lumber,
slatted, without a thatch, is numbered,
hand-stacked. In the east, a bay sniffs
a star-headed filly. Hoofs beat on red clay.

Shoes shush over crushed stone paths. Apple
slices crunch between horse teeth.
Airplanes crosshatching sluices of exhaust
pass over poplar leaves shuttering in a surly

breeze. A red-skinned man pipes music
to his ears. A woman's dark eye once caught,
never unhooks from his. And nowhere
a straight nail. No one cares. A flicker left early.

Goodbye

The parrots say "goodbye."
Salamanders signal the health of a system.
Miners trust fierce
singing in the dark.
The parrot says "goodbye"
to the snow leopard,
spots vanishing into the scrub,
into the white dust
of our long winter night.
The salamander, shape-shifter,
signals the health of the system.
Let no one find you,
snowy owl.
Let no one track you,
mountain gorilla, sniff
your droppings, feed
on what you leave behind.
Parrots are costly
to capture and breed.
Salamander signals the health of the system.
So much depends
upon those changing colors.
The parrot says "goodbye"
in English, Spanish, and Chinese.
We've taught our parrot well.

Erasure

The possibility of saying something becomes more
difficult. The urgency of saying nothing rings the ears.
Moving forward is definitely an option,
while the tendency to backpedal

must be considerable. Now bears
roam our backyards. In our
barbecue pits, we sift no ashes, no sooty remnants
of designer wood chips, smoky and delicious.

Some prefer surreal yet unremarkable
buffalo. No one speaks of ostrich.
It was supposed to be
my last questioning moment, my final

shimmy up the wrong
family tree. Some call it Natural Extinction:
If you can whiz on tender tiger lily shoots,
the deer won't eat them.

My father said soulfully, "It takes two to tango."
And before you could say Jack Rabbit,
a giant hole opened in our heart pine floor, just polished,
a rectangle devoid of…a grand sucking canyon of a . . .

sinkhole or a sieve, much like a giant colander not catching
the spaghetti. You were kind of dressed wrong
for the occasion, in Grandfather's tux, shirtless,
sporting a tiara. So what if nobody asked me.

>

Seven ants and counting,
the ninth took the high road, gingerly exploring
the kitchen ceiling, as you found
a newspaper and started rolling it up.

Lonely Horse Galaxy

"That horse is lonely," my father announced,
visiting the farm after my marriage collapsed.
Patriot kept chewing alfalfa.
I fed him cornhusks, apples from my palm,
petted him like the dog I'd given up.

"That horse is lonely," my father repeated,
leaning on the white fence, poking
his head into the field to focus
more poignancy on horse feelings.
Patriot trotted neither toward nor away.

"That horse is lonely." My father sighed
a big sigh. Am I going crazy, I wondered;
hasn't he said that before?
My father knew nothing about daughters,
a little about horses, cut off from the herd.

Ghost Horses and the Morning Sky

Bright planets to the east, north, northeast,
split the difference. One doesn't find skies

like this. Cassiopeia, Thuban in Draco, Ursa Minor
visible along with Orion's belt and bow,

bent by an arrow, forever notched.
And when it flings will this sky unhinge,

Andromeda our terra firma again?
I have fewer and fewer names for what I can see.

On the earth, in the nearby field,
I think I hear horses stirring the limbs

of October-bearing Osage Orange, of Walnut,
scrubby Virginia pines, and Juniper.

The horses' ridged backs, knobs of spine
between fat flanks, find planet light, and shine.

My eyes transfix as feet shuffle pebbles,
sun not far behind my journey.

I can see my hands and feet when white
laces blink. Keeping to the path, I skirt the dew.

Above me this sky opens in the moment, an immense
thought caught in creation's throat.

May a poet still use words like these? I know
the answer is *no*.

Backward Glance

Dragging the ghost of the trees in my tarp, I look to stripped limbs'
jagged outlines against a clouded atmosphere.

My heavy-lidded day smells of mold and leaves slick with rot.
I should leave rumination alone, but I remember

how the deer's contortionist repose betrayed it.
Death first appeared at the edge of the bathroom mirror

while I brushed my teeth. A shift of focus from my own grin
to the torque of tawny neck over lean hock and foreleg

stretched my imagination and later my strength.
The deer's position on a mossy bed, the cleanliness of a fresh smile,

every tooth in my head a glistening measure, a scraped
memento mori. Like these leaves, the deer was pulled on a green

tarp, tipped onto eager earth away from the mirror's distortion
and toward the turkey buzzards.

Homeless Galaxy

Drifting countries with Lord Karma
on my Saturn return, that ol' American

feeling fucked up and doomed.
Too many worlds make up each human.

To this mutt of the brave and free,
great-grandmother Kasey seals a green mystery.

On the other side, resolute, reliable, or *estalee*,
an Old French fishtrap or one who fishes.

Under the twin-headed eagle's empiric feet
lie several centuries of mercenary energies,

Protestants fleeing popes, or wait, wait, do tell:
Captain John Smith led us from Old Bohemia

across Europe, Britain, and choppy seas
to Jamestown oozing nebulas of DNA.

In border places Druids and Jews brewed
crude liquor in the caldron of my blood.

Cedar

To hail from nowhere is a resonate gift.
It means you can be anywhere. It means I can be here.

Saw through the curved branch, fibrous
bark sinew-wrapped as wisteria vine,

and unseal the waft that will knock you down.
Its scent a stain of blood. Insect

proof. Divinely inspired.
To work with hands a length of life

into a shape of use is no small thing. My connections
fail.

The wood stuns me with its power
even in dying.

The Buffalo Return

Grandfather, the banker,
gave bribes for scripted answers.

Buffalo nickels, two-dollar bills,
birthday silver dollars,
Kennedy fifty cents,
Mr. Hamilton's crooked grin.

What will you do with all of your money?
"Put it in the bank," I said my part.

All they did as a couple was yell.
Grandmother's garden
grew in messy tiers
of velvet purple/yellow pansies.

I jimmied her miniature safe
stuffed with greenbacks.
Somewhere in compost
she'd misplaced the key.

"Don't pay him any mind," she said,
ninety years, hands over her ears.

Galaxy of Virginia History

"The worst insult in my thirty years,"
the teacher said. Arms flapping,
she turned from the board

to her brood.
Open on our desks, the Virginia History
fourth grade text.

Exhibit A: an ink drawing of a slave ship
approaching land,
brown arms and heads

poking from the hold toward air.
Exaggerations of smiling teeth
set for a birthday party.

The caption read
that arriving Africans "jumped for joy"
upon seeing

the Virginia shores…
In 1967, I raised my hand to ask
if those words were really fact.

Echoes

The spherical universe has been other things:
A flat central earth encircled by the sun.

Expanding infinitely, dark matter pushes us apart.
Fierce dragons swim the map's legend.

A hole in our atmosphere breathes silent gas.
By cultural consensus, fear, like war, can be useful.

Meteorites fell in a Russian forest—dinosaurs collapsed.
The comet circled back to claim you and me.

A cold dead hand thrust skyward from the earth's crust.
Your ankle crumpled first, then your heart.

I never knew what hit us as you erupted in a solar flare.
This pincushion universe echoes, light stabbed.

Conquistadors in the Colonies

To be constantly reminded of who won the war.
To be constantly reminded that the conquerors
are good. That their intentions are loving.

To walk outside and observe a couple of cardinals,
to listen to their song remembering
the appropriation of song, the suppression

of certain tongues, the oppressor's constant struggle
to overcome the cardinals, to locate their nest
before the eggs open. Or to condition their children

to fly with their heads looking over their shoulders.
One flew backwards. One flew into a windowpane.
One could never learn. It was slow.

Someone said, "They're all like that."
Someone else nodded.

z8_GND_5296

Bored in school,
I practiced drawing
                    boxes
built from sorted

rectangles
            pitched at diagonals,
like large and small dippers
connected by four lines.

From a simple
formula,
I derived a number
of variants:

            black boxes,
ballot boxes, boom boxes,
box seats, air boxes,
juke boxes, batter's boxes,

old console TV's, caskets,
ears that had been righteously
boxed, long rose boxes
to hold the world's

distant blessings,
boîte vitesse, boîte postale,
boxes strong enough to bear
blunt questions,

boxes so encoded
I had to use smaller
& smaller hands
holding miniscule,

invisible pencils
minus erasers.
Inside 700 million
years of space,

objects & light, of course,
wear masks.
Extinct hydrogen gas
                    disguises

the birth of new stars,
                    now ancient,
recently mourned,
fallen hostage to old red blurs.

Not Einstein

The father and the mother were neither smiling nor alone.

And their children were not at home. All five enjoyed pizza, not pasta or antipasto, neither steaming nor raw, and one of them unacknowledged but nonetheless there: the only one not frowning. You might say his mind waxed with imagination, replacing well-traveled synapses with crackling old radio storms. This one was not going to be a surgeon or an engineer or a famous author, this much was clear.

He was not headed for adventure, trawling or trading. He was not going places. Was he gliding like a flying fish? He was not. I would say he was not quite right, and yet, as he ate, the only one not frowning, the only one not disconnected from the chatter in the air and the drumming music around him, I thought it was the parents who were not all there.

The mother crossed her arms, not smoking. That was not *her* son. The father only had eyes for his other ones, nothing wrong with either of them; they were not addled or ugly or tuneful. Their mouths did not hang open; they were not nearly full-grown and stuck at the table's foot. These parents were not loving all three, loving only two, were most obviously not loving

the only one not frowning.

Ice Convoy

It traveled through the dark
only when I was sleeping.

A floe over barren tundra—
a glacier in the making, marked

by lava gravel—hinged
from nowhere to nowhere.

This energy snake carried cargo.
A line of army Jeeps traversed it.

My black car loaded
with you and me jumped

topics, crossing a cold barrier
of deep winter scrapings to find the road.

My tires climbed jagged chunks of snow
like white plates someone threw

in frustration. We skidded into line
to join the convoy. Our tires spun

on ice, dredging quick-sands
of glassy slush, and no one

behind us could progress. I gripped
the wheel when the burning smell

commenced, and you never said
where you wanted us to go.

No Galaxy

In the No galaxy a poem
waits to be written
a hen sits an egg
that won't hatch
pies never cool in the safe
and hay is neither cut nor baled
it merely grows
in the No galaxy
we were never friends
I neglected to welcome you in
you never called again
or even once
there's nothing to see
but a small pinpoint diminishing
from a bomb not dropped
from a bi-plane disappeared
we were never here
thus with air trees water and breeze
oh the sea does foam against the shore
and a pelican plop
sea ducks dive and bottom up
yet in the larger sense nothing happens
back in the countryside
no trout no pole no lure no hole
no camping no chimp in space
no composure
no curiosity no rain not a cloud
nothin' doing not on my watch
not perfect not in my backyard
marriage not
no sound in the forest

mystery solved
children not country not
no pain

Invasion

I fear ants in my food.
They terrorize with quizzical
patterns, tiny hammers,
wood screws. They invite
free-loaders to freckle my floors,
doorways, drains,
banana skins, bare toes.

I cripple some ants.
I don't mean to, but I do.
Others I squash flat
leaving one liquid dot
beneath each creature
like a wandering third eye,
an omega caste mark.

I slip ten *corpora delicti*
into a business envelope,
bless them, seal their paper
tomb with kisses tiny and wet,
iron the paste with my fist,
address it to the federation
of what doesn't return.

Bee Tree

A bee colony,
black hole
in a split juniper trunk.
Gnarled, rough mounds of bark
guard a slash of buzzing dark.

Wild bees delight,
work and hover—
dive into an artificial night.
They pass each other
to cover cones with stolen nectar.

This could be the last bee tree
in a food chain of cultivated
colonies. Bee homebodies
thrive—imports mingle
without improvement,

and migrants sicken, shipped
on flatbeds cross-country.
No swarm, only purposeful acts
in a daylong dance to and fro.
The gash of hive is low

on the trunk, the whole
secret two feet high.
This fir, bearing cones
like shrunken blueberries,
with bark striations of whitish grey,

resembles a faded fence post
more than a living tree.
Inside there is a kingdom
waiting to collapse
on a queen so plump with life

she cannot see the danger
of such sweetness. Expanding
honey cores the juniper,
as sinkholes honeycomb the comet's
nucleus until it cries out,

its coma burning bigger than Jupiter.
17P/Holmes explodes gas
and dust as sun strikes it.
To the eye, a fuzzy spot enlivens
Perseus. To the lazy

bees, tucked into a moon-lit tree
it is nothing. Soon, it is nothing.

Shakespeare Galaxy

....If the universe is infinitely big, then the number of distinct
configurations of particles will have to repeat.
—Brian Greene

Exhumed from a dripping cave
still in formation,
sealed in clay jars, it was
carried by donkey down rocky paths
to a scientific hut draped with sun-blocking
parachute cloth.

The paleontologist
peers up from his bone cache
in diffuse tent light
to crack a jar with his chisel
and uncork with pliers
               the last shard of text.

Etched on papyrus: tragedy, history,
each comedy with sides splitting
and curling, the complete works
of a Shakespeare hitherto unknown.
Oh God I could be bounded
in a nutshell, and count myself. . . .

The manuscripts appear to date
from a time prior to a time
out of joint, long before England,
Ben Johnson or Maxwell, back to a storied era
when dinosaurs were great thinkers
and infinite space itself king.

So, who has been this other Shakespeare,
this impostor, simulacrum, bad dream,
this prince of twisting syntax?
Whose stinging hackwork
have we sown through centuries,
what smiling villain have we not slain?

And after this seminal Shakespeare,
of course another Shakespeare
is waiting to emerge. Our legacy besmeared
and besmirched, nothing but endless
plagiarized chestnuts stuck in memory,
copies of copies, copies of copies.

Famous Brains

"There's something I have to tell you. Sorry," I said,
"but I do. It won't take forever, but it's important."

"Don't worry," you said.
"The Osage orange trees will bloom a certain
blop of brain-like fruit and drop it
all along this path come October.
You'll just be walking, but your course
will alter." I opened my mouth.
"October," you said. "Lime green. Trust me."

"Did you know
there's a brain bank with famous
right hemispheres preserved in
formaldehyde?
And freezers full of slices?"

"Whose?" you asked.
Finally, I had your attention.

Head of Sappho

We cannot know his legendary head
  —Rainer Maria Rilke, "Archaic Torso of Apollo"

As a thousand maple leaves deflect,
times ten as many branches flutter.
Along the river, bridges reflect
the slow slide of evening's sails,

and I remember you, at least your
giant head, severed at the neck,
served up on the Roman marble floor
in Istanbul. So many other bards
twist their voices with yours and stuff
words in your mouth, those bastards,

but they cannot kiss the full honey
without leaning close to your lyre.
Entwining ivy curls your hair. Confess
to me what you see in your long stare

of exile, old age, I'm straining to hear—
Sappo sapp, What's happening, Baby?
Your image stamped six different coins
of the realm, Tenth Muse and clearest.

There must be more than crumbling nose
for trouble here—*whiter than an egg*—.
You said, *I am dissolved—my tongue useless—
ears ring—I am little better than dead*—.
My love for you, my Giant Fragment,
Dear, can't but grow in your body's absence.   >

37

In silence, Figment, my fervor restored,
I am *fiction weaving* ever more.

Galaxy of the Courthouse Steps

Quilt stitched from grandfather's silk ties,
variations of light and dark Log Cabin.
Wherever one looks, one sees more

and more steps, more or less
amounts of justice to mete.
The guilty pray for leniency

beside the innocent. On the courthouse
steps a young man waits to be
called. Your grandmother,

then young, heads past to pay a tax.
Their eyes connect. He's a character
witness in his friend's rape trial.

This organic pattern turns geometric,
sheep studded on a steep hillside
tumbling for lack of the crook.

This man, this witness, is neither guilty
nor innocent. He is your grandfather.
Complicit, your blood flows with his.

The Hat and Heart Quilt

The hat must depart.
The heart stays for breakfast.

The hat prepares for rain.
The heart stretches in a warm spot of sun.

The hat explodes, a star.
The heart unwinds a ball of twine.

The hat waits for tomorrow.
The heart fails to flower.

The hat floats in the current.
The heart sinks in cement boots.

The hat acts as a fan in hot weather.
The heart flails, a kite stuck in wires.

The hat fits neat, corners creased.
The heart sends a written message.

The hat knows too much.
The heart, like the stomach, is stuffed.

The hat cipher displays only its shape.
The heart reveals all in trying to escape.

The hat will never be a train.
The heart will never be erased.

The hat has had its last hoorah.
The ashes of the heart catch wind and fly.

The Bridge

It's true that the bridge owns almost nothing. Not even the river. The river keeps, bestows, rises, floods, follows, retreats. As for what the bridge sees, it is somewhat limited by its stationary perspective, by its spanning the same width of water, irrevocably. Water's nature is to be always moving, yet from the bridge the river forms a constant, like X. The tumbling X-water may as well be the water of yesterday, today, and tomorrow. Imagine the bridge with its eyes closed and arms raised, a drawbridge unfolding like an eagle soaring. Now the bridge is asleep. No one passes on foot or by wheel. The bridge, good somnambulist, stays open to suggestion, and makes an easy subject for a hypnotist. I tried a past-life regression on the bridge. It saw nothing. I asked the bridge to imagine its birth. The bridge shook violently. I asked the bridge to imagine its mother. The bridge sighed, losing balance, beginning to swing. I asked the bridge to open its eyes and tell me everything it saw. Even the river X stopped moving then. It was as if the iron bridge vanished and the river receded from its usual path, both river and bridge ripped from the visible. I had to imagine the words for myself, words instead of X's for what the bridge might choose to name. The bridge, once *my* bridge and now gone, commenced to howl.

Galaxy of the Fathers

The fathers slog home from work tired,
ready for some chow.

The fathers are cheered in the uniform
of their country.

The fathers walk into a bar and order rotgut
shots in an Old West movie.

The fathers always earn their promotions.

The fathers return home injured, requiring
constant long-term care.

The proud fathers sport broad smiles.

The fathers take a day off and play golf,
bait a hook, shoot some hoops.

The brave fathers are decorated.

The fathers sacrifice their only sons.

The angry fathers decide to bail.

The fathers write a Declaration and sign it
with a flourish.

The fathers are afforded every opportunity.

The fathers take to the streets and grow
long hair.

The fathers are selfless.

The fathers are prayed to on a daily basis.

The fathers attempt some humor.

The fathers invade other fathers.

The fathers mutter about how everyone
is out to get them.

The fathers are anguished geniuses.

The fathers win large sums of money
for their *craft or sullen art.*

The fathers never have enough.

The fathers take medication prescribed
by other fathers.

The fathers say that standards are being eroded.

The fathers serve as final judges.

90-day Wonder

Something you had been meaning to say
a cause and a perfection
a reason for being
underwater
wearing a mask and snorkel
sailing by sextant
he almost failed navigation
in South Bend Indiana
two pilots downed in the waters
in front of the ship
it swerved to avoid them
but their charges
detonated upon hitting their depths
rocking the cradle
floating the dead
a cause célèbre
a plume of uncertain origin
on their shakedown cruise
just out of the harbor
they hit a whale
sixty feet in length
the bow sliced its spine twice
it came up in chunks
a bloody wake and some pieces of proof
they did not run aground
two pilots bounding across the deck
slo-mo bomb tilted from an enemy
wing
falling below the flight deck and into
unventilated quarters
of CVE-70

a little Kaiser coffin
well named at that moment
it takes five generations to produce
thunderous grease fires
blew unidentifiable bodies
in parts
sky high
one of the pilots kept running
without his head
the other one turned
and saw it
a war to end all wars
a shining example
that's what he was called
Schizophrenic
of unseasonable warmth
the lake is usually cold at this time of year
the ocean can change in a moment
wearing a belt and suspenders
I tried on his mid-shipman's
bell bottoms with button fronts
a shining example
of unwarranted affection
after twenty odd years
it strafes a village
it was nothing anyone wanted
the moths had left the wool alone
and nonetheless a suppression
above all else
Combustible Vulnerable Expendable
a 90-day Wonder
in a salty dog's war

Mental Casualty

Distant and undone,
he shuffled the ward, cigarette
between stained finger and thumb.

He had been there
in 1948, again in '51,

feeling the burn of nightmare,
day sweats, restraining straps,
on a Thursday full of woe

and insulin shock. I thought
"The Veteran's . . ." meant
the veterans, the men.

This man, our father, came back
limbs intact, not a hero
on a float of tissue roses.

If he had better tolerated war,
he might have served us
better as a father.

He counted all of his remaining years:
"When your number's up,
your number's up."

The call returns. He's not here.
He volunteered.

Galaxy of Waiting

Waiting at the firehouse doors,
enumerating hoof marks from a former age. Waiting
for steel wheels to flatten a coin on the rails,
so that it looks like a disk minted by eons of pressure. Waiting
for the Exodus and the Red Sea. Waiting for the reruns
of antiquity when returning gods favor the other side. Waiting
for laundry to wash and then dry. Waiting for irony
to stop being so ironic, and for cynics to rot.
Waiting for a taste of honey. Waiting for a taste
of the strong leaf tea of victory. Waiting for the lapse
of judgment concerning the past several centuries to abate.
Waiting for an end to sorrow. Waiting for inspiration.
Waiting for the Republic to ring true,
pressed against the glass ceiling, under the harsh light
of yesterday, played again and again like there's no tomorrow.
Waiting at red for green promises. Waiting and waiting,
waiting for reason to prevail, waiting for planting season. Waiting
for the apocalypse and the white horses, and so forth.
Waiting for the cyst to shrink. Waiting for a phone
call, waiting for Christmas, the next stall, clerk, or straw.
Waiting for rebates, waiting for apologies. Waiting in pajamas.
Waiting in negligees. Waiting for the apiaries to buzz again
with bees. Waiting for a stellar performance. Waiting
for a good series. Waiting for a drop in the bucket. Waiting
on rooftops for rescue. Waiting in 100 degree heat while the waters
rise around us. Waiting until some of us die and others
start wading through the muck. Waiting for the
alligators while we wrestle sharks. Waiting for plastic
to break down in the waters. Waiting for Exxon
to pay for the largest spill in history. Waiting for reports
from the various branches which will confirm and support

what was previously suspected, accounted for,
and secretly installed as policy. Waiting for
an election. Waiting for lunch. Waiting for an oil change.
Waiting for some people to shut up and for others
to act up and speak up. Waiting for the kids at school,
parked on the circle with the other
mothers. Waiting for the bus after work with the folks
who take the bus. Waiting for that guy who always cracks
us up to do so again, while we're standing here, waiting.
Waiting for Walt Whitman to stop making so much sense.
Waiting for a raise. Waiting for a compliment. Waiting for an insider
stock tip. Waiting for others to stop whining. Waiting for
the rest of creation to see it our way. Waiting for the bootstrappers
to line up and just shoot the rest of us with
automatics, since we're so slow,
wasteful, and ignorant of the rules. Waiting for justice. Waiting
for just cause. Waiting for the Medal of Honor long after you're buried,
habeas corpus. Because you are an American Indian and all records
of your valor lost or incinerated, and the statute of limitations
has run out on your claim. Waiting for the horses to return,
and the firehouse doors to burst open
and a thunderous clattering ensue, pulling behind
it the answer to our many prayers, the water of conciliation,
the spiritual balm of healing, the baptism that feels like swimming,
the swimming that carries us all to the other shore.

Waiting for Darkness Visible

Not Milton's darkness visible,
but something more mundane
that happens in the time it takes
for rods to supersede cones.

I am not used to waiting. By choice,
I would do almost anything else:
effect a shopping list,
turn a screw with the wrong

driver stripping the head.
Anything but this, this, this.
I admit, a lot has been written
around the theme, even a touchstone

of twentieth century drama.
Meanwhile, there's a path before me
covered in the fur of darkness
not brightening a bit. By Friday

this ripened moon will end the mystery
of where to place my feet.
Here in Indian summer relief,
waiting for the World Series to begin,

waiting for a break in the boredom,
I lift my head, as if from a book:
Venus flares up and the map of night sky
hurtles over me, not waiting for me to look.

May Meteors

If clouds clear before dawn, we'll see remnants of Halley's
dust ripping the sky.

If we wake in time, we'll monitor the spectacle for the peak hour
during the dim new moon.

If all continues as planned, we can endure the crick in our necks
to taste the crisp air of spring.

The back door opens, we tiptoe outside, and there's a warning growl.
The black bear tenders its ritual

down the muddy mountainside. The train whistles and wheels,
rattling the whole valley below.

Cotton clouds scrim bright orbs, hide Aquarius high in the southeast.
If we are patient,

if we are good, if we are silent, if we are amenable, if we are waiting
we never arrive.

Galaxy of Six Women

The creature grand and gone,
hard to leave alone—

A paleontologist hefts fossils
from bonebeds, from long rocky slumbers.

In the mirror, eyes focus
on themselves. Right as left,

left as right. Any intelligent
being would be dying out.

My hair turns from black
to white as I check my watch.

Native Americans north, central
and south carry six women

whose mitochondria DNA
crossed Beringia, the land bridge

submerged some 20,000 years.
Their traces mark 95 percent.

Two men walk barefoot in the sky, clouds
torn in their wake. I wish their feet

were mine. I believe in rooftops,
in wind, workmen hammering.

>

The damn pigeons shiver
my shoulders with their dreaded

yammering. My family tree must
have its end. Chattering children launch

a striped sail in the sea. A guitar
echoes sweet chords. Clouds

or men endure in giant steps.
My mother's voice stops with me.

Slavish Devotion

Each Sunday we visited with snips,
a tin pail half of water,
half of garden blooms.

I followed, followed
the motions of the elders, the aunts
who never matriculated from home.

At the cemetery, they knew just where
they were going, straight
to the mausoleum, their names

already engraved, an open date
with eternity. They
threw out last week's putrid mess

of shriveled roses and ferns, refreshed
the flora in the brass urn
and told me stories

of the ancestors who lived
in the wall.
My grandfather's heart

stopped after dinner
before I was born.
My invalid grandmother,

their stepmother,
raised them "like her own."
Their tone was reverential

and sometimes they cried.
If you asked me what we worshiped
then, I would have said "Grandmother,"

not any god or god's son
whose most important moments
were spent dying.

One Girl's Discoveries

Galaxies of women...
　　　—Adrienne Rich, "Planetarium"

A sky-gazing child, intrigued
by constellations and stormy weather,
tornadoes and ripe tomatoes,
Lisa announced over fruit loops
her aspiration to join NASA.

A. Mother said, "Stop, you're a girl."
B. Mother said, "But I never went to college."
C. Mother said, "That's crazy."
D. Mother said, "Shoot for the stars."
E. None of the above.

At nineteen, she discovered AGC#310842.
She said, "People expect me to be older."
Lisa traveled to Arecibo, Puerto Rico,
to the world's largest radio telescope.
Awaiting confirmation: five other galaxies.

Data the young woman ponders
are older than she will ever be.
Lisa maintains rapt fascination
for physics and meteorology.
(The answer is D.)

Glass Galaxy

The world: Glass, swirls of color, irregular sine waves so distinctly interwoven that to wonder at the hard surface was to miss the liquid nature of the internal construction. I hardly knew you, yet I gave you this world, a swirl your palm could cup. I wanted to see if you could keep it from breaking. I wanted to see you hold it to your eye, a scientist's piercing observant eye that measured smoke into beakers. Your blue shots of sight, your ice-infused acknowledgments could shatter. Initially the object's beauty captured you, or the thought of a solid elixir. Unlikely for a season of cards and chocolate boxes, an artist's planet, a galaxy of temperaments' collision, combustion of a brief and lasting nature.

A chemical compound fused on the day I saw you without knowing who you were: My skin struck fire.

Not nostalgia now, not mistakenly undone, hijacked, but more or less a harkening that never rang true, a course that never finished but which left a rupture in a single slipknot, gnawed and raveled. Spring run aground, water halted, reins to a horse's gallop. Full stop to the soft mouth, a pause, an extended musical rest written to settle a score. That can never be evened. The glass world, a manufactured eye simulating flesh was marvelous, yet the thing lost equaled so much more than its replacement.

The thing erased was living: That world we made was made to break and break.

Lizard

...a panting lizard/waited for history...
—William Stafford, "At the Bomb Testing Site"

Black blood and chemical sunsets
from the nuclear power plant
near Auvillar, our quaint southern village,
a pretty bit of evidence stirring up
windstorms, thunder puffs that never
erupt. A cannon fires into the sky

to ward off lightning and hellfire.
Black bloodlines, small veins
of iron traverse a mineral hunk.
Prometheus grew a daily liver
only to suffer its being plucked
from his side and eaten by an eagle.

In Eastern Europe the hazelnuts,
contaminated by Chernobyl
well into the next century,
glow like the water. Not fit, it will
turn stomachs, blacken pink bowels
and wilt everything within them.

Milk-painted green shutters
work against sun in even gestures.
A cool breeze limits
contentment, limits joy, limits
pleasure, limits anger and all the furies.
The buzzing of plump flies

reminds me of the daily news,
of how everything can be or have a corpse,
an eye that blinks, a downside,
flipside, memory, a lurid spin.
I was trying not to wake during my
lifetime and wondering

how I got where I got,
the hours, the continents, the river
spillage from hard rains rumbling past.
The woman told her story
of rejection, how her parents
murdered her tie to them.

She pushed us off, dropping
word bombs.
We stopped listening.
A split screen glimpse of oneself:
I was caught, a five-lined skink,
half dull brown, half measured

by my indigo, shining tail—
that severed and squirmed
and will re-grow. Comets
touted doomsday at the ends
of several centuries in a row.
False alarms resound.

Warm sunlight on brick
brings out the lizards.
Darkness, roaches.
Morning, the local newspaper.
Evening, the moonflowers bloom.
In the village the clock chimes

steady half-hour intervals.
At 13:30 the postmistress
reopens for a second half day.
*Bonjour, madame, je voudrais
trois carte postal pour l'etais-unis,
s'il vous plait, merci, merci.*

Endtimes

2012
The rooster crows, and the world is not ending
as long as *la Garonne* flows red,
not from blood but clay, the crumbling
earth that rolls downhill when it pours.

Mud that makes pots cure in Gascony kilns
supplies elephants their vitamins
on the sun-baked veldt
and grows generations of elephant kin.

What cannot be seen is dark energy
plus dark matter, in theory,
with neither emission nor reflection.
We're living in the four percent zone,

our narrow band of the directly known.
What can we accomplish within our scant
percentage, our fractional existence?
This is no time for ceremony, indeed.

The sun beats down on straw heads.
Our only worry is the eastern thunder.
Sampling every lace of green and root,
we wander as though it's forever.

11:11

The rooster crows, and the world is not ending
as long as ginger can be grated
into beets and stirred,
garlic smashed into butter with

wild morels and a dash of olive oil.
My grandmother's dank root cellar,
lined with jars of persimmon and apricot,
smelled of gasoline from the mower,

fresh divots churned by the rear wheels.
To the Maya, the Milky Way
meant a road of souls, the route
to the underworld = our passage to heaven.

9:11

Our solar system is slated to pause in eclipse
at the galaxy's middle. Earth's magnetic
poles will shift, reverse. Foretold,
this has not happened yet.

If all time is equally present, can it stop?
Can we stop this time, this time past?
The polar bear finds her footing,
afloat with her cub. The planes

never crash and the towers hold fast.
There was a time when this did not happen.
There was a chance this did not happen.
There was a reversal of fortune.

Before the final divination
from the codified books of God
that beset man on man, wax figures
trapped in strata of igneous

rock still await eruption.
The clattering shark's tooth necklace
makes a sound like regret.
There's no going back on this lying net.

5:55
The rooster is crowing, and the world is not ending.
All day and night the rooster
wails, as though he were in Spain
or Mexico, where roosters never sleep.

The crowing has crossed borders.
There are no national songs the rooster knows.
There are no love songs the rooster knows.
There was a time when this rooster

was a pet, but the cold man sold him.
Now he cannot stop telling his woe.
The albatross has nothing on this blubbering,
this dingy red comb badge of dishonor.

4:44
The rusty feathers of the rooster shine
after the storm. His mate, the white chicken
up the hill, perches on a split fence rung.
What to do with these signs and portents?

When the clock says 11:11 every time
you look. When the dash reads 5:55
with 55 mile per hour road signs
framing the car in traffic, multiplying

the 5's luck. When the digits are 4:44
every night you cannot sleep.
When everywhere you look the clocks
are ticking past 2012. I unfurl

the tourist Mayan calendar
from San Miguel, study the symbols
around the painted wheel.
Planets, stars, seasons, crops, and time.

Stars sighted by sextant measure
location at sea. Space and time, once
necessarily linked, parted for several
centuries awaiting Einstein.

10:10
There's mystery in what numbers
come up for you. Some swear by
7's. Others claim 13 for their jerseys.
Parents favor their children's natal

combinations, as though those
accidents will unlock Godspeed
at the track. I won the lottery
on a hunch on my sister's birthday

and felt showered with envy after
the billboard announcement.
Luck = the most outrageous achievement.
Forget fallout shelters. Pray for luck.

Erased Galaxy

After De Kooning aftermath
after Rauschenberg
afterthought
after 1957 afterglow
after the Edsel happily ever
after the party aftereffect
after the storm afterbirth

when you clean up your room
when the war ends
when pigs fly
when hell freezes over
when I get off the phone
when you grow up
when I get around to it whenever

to beat the band
to a post to understand
to stay together toward
to you to the skin
to beat a dead horse
to me to the matter at hand
to my taste to wit

without warning world
without end without regret
without knowledge
without the dog without a clue
without thinking goes
without saying without fear
without excuse

until the cows come home
until it boils
until payday
until tomorrow
until I see you again
until the flour is just damp
until death do us part

where you found out
where we left off
where she is to blame
where we are from
where we went wrong
where what never was meets what's not to be
whereupon